Hold Christmas in Your Heart

African-American Songs, Poems, and
Stories for the Holidays

compiled by Cheryl Willis Hudson

Cartwheel
·B·O·O·K·S· ®

SCHOLASTIC INC.

New York Toronto London Auckland Sydney

We gratefully acknowledge the writers and illustrators listed below for their contributions to this publication. Every effort has been made to trace the ownership of all copyrighted material and to secure permission to reprint these selections. In the event of any question arising as to the use of any material, the editor and the publisher, while expressing regret for any inadvertent error, will be happy to make the necessary correction in future printings.

It's Christmas in the House! by Mia Watson, illustrated by Anna Rich. Text copyright © 1995 by Mia Watson. Illustration copyright © 1995 by Anna Rich. Text reprinted by permission of Mia Watson. Illustration reprinted by permission of Anna Rich.

Tradition by Gwendolyn Brooks, illustrated by Cal Massey. Text copyright © 1993 by Gwendolyn Brooks, reprinted from *Maud Martha*, Chicago: Third World Press, 1993. Illustration copyright © 1995 by Cal Massey. Illustration reprinted by permission of Cal Massey.

My Christmas Tree by Gertrude Parthenia McBrown, illustrated by Eric Battle. Text copyright © 1935 by Gertrude Parthenia McBrown, originally published in *The Picture-Poetry Book*, copyright © 1935, renewed 1968 by The Associated Publishers, Inc., Washington, DC. Text reprinted by permission of The Associated Publishers, Inc. Illustration copyright © 1995 by Eric Battle. Illustration reprinted by permission of Eric Battle.

Midnight Service by Marguerita Roett, illustrated by James Ransome. Text copyright © 1995 by Marguerita Roett. Illustration copyright © 1995 by James Ransome. Text reprinted by permission of Marguerita Roett. Illustration reprinted by permission of James Ransome.

Go, Tell It on the Mountain adapted and arranged by John W. Work III, illustrated by Ron Garnett. Music arrangement copyright © by John W. Work III, reprinted by permission of Mrs. John W. Work III. Illustration copyright © 1995 by Ron Garnett. Illustration reprinted by permission of Ron Garnett.

Snow by Angela Shelf Medearis, illustrated by Sylvia Walker. Text copyright © 1995 by Angela Shelf Medearis. Illustration copyright © 1995 by Sylvia Walker. Text reprinted by permission of Angela Shelf Medearis. Illustration reprinted by permission of Sylvia Walker.

From *Everett Anderson's Year* by Lucille Clifton, illustrated by Sylvia Walker. Text copyright © 1974 by Lucille Clifton. Reprinted by permission of Henry Holt and Company, Inc. Illustration copyright © Sylvia Walker. Illustration reprinted by permission of Sylvia Walker.

Brer Rabbit's Christmas Gift retold by Mia Watson, illustrated by Eric Battle. Text copyright © 1995 by Mia Watson. Illustration copyright © 1995 by Eric Battle. Text reprinted by permission of Mia Watson. Illustration reprinted by permission of Eric Battle.

Christmas Kittens by Cheryl Willis Hudson, illustrated by Higgins Bond. Text copyright © 1995 by Cheryl Willis Hudson. Illustration copyright © 1995 by Higgins Bond. Text reprinted by permission of Cheryl Willis Hudson. Illustration reprinted by permission of Higgins Bond.

Carol of the Brown King by Langston Hughes, illustrated by Cal Massey. Text from *Collected Poems by Langston Hughes*, copyright © by the Estate of Langston Hughes. Reprinted by permission of Alfred A. Knopf, Inc. Illustration copyright © 1995 by Cal Massey. Illustration reprinted by permission of Cal Massey.

Children, Go Where I Send Thee, traditional Black carol, illustrated by Anna Rich. Illustration copyright © 1995 by Anna Rich. Illustration reprinted by permission of Anna Rich.

California Christmas by Toyomi Igus, illustrated by Ron Garnett. Text copyright © 1995 by Toyomi Igus. Illustration copyright © 1995 by Ron Garnett. Text reprinted by permission of Toyomi Igus. Illustration reprinted by permission of Ron Garnett.

Christmas Valentine by Nikki Grimes, illustrated by Cal Massey. Text copyright © 1995 by Nikki Grimes. Illustration copyright © 1995 by Cal Massey. Text reprinted by permission of Nikki Grimes. Illustration reprinted by permission of Cal Massey.

Shepherd's Song at Christmas by Langston Hughes, illustrated by Ron Garnett. Text from *Collected Poems by Langston Hughes*, copyright © by the Estate of Langston Hughes. Reprinted by permission of Alfred A. Knopf, Inc. Illustration copyright © 1995 by Ron Garnett. Illustration reprinted by permission of Ron Garnett.

Christmas is a-comin' by Huddie Ledbetter, illustrated by Anna Rich. *Christmas is Coming (Almost Day)*, new words and new music by Huddie Ledbetter TRO — copyright © 1951 (renewed) and 1959 (renewed) Folkways Music Publishers, Inc., New York, NY. Used by permission. Illustration copyright © 1995 by Anna Rich. Illustration reprinted by permission of Anna Rich.

New Year's Wish by Cheryl Willis Hudson, illustrated by Cal Massey. Text copyright © 1995 by Cheryl Willis Hudson. Text reprinted by permission of Cheryl Willis Hudson. Illustration copyright © 1995 by Cal Massey. Illustration reprinted by permission of Cal Massey.

**Hold Christmas in Your Heart: African-American Songs,
Poems, and Stories for the Holidays**
ISBN 0-590-48024-3
Cheryl Willis Hudson, compiler.
All rights reserved. Published by Scholastic Inc.
by arrangement with Just Us Books, Inc.
CARTWHEEL BOOKS and the CARTWHEEL BOOKS logo
are registered trademarks of Scholastic Inc.

Library of Congress Cataloging-in-Publication Data
Hold Christmas in your heart: African-American songs, poems, and
  stories for the holidays / compiled by Cheryl Willis Hudson.
    p. cm.
  Summary: Many of the selections are by African-American authors
(Langston Hughes, Lucille Clifton) and all of the illustrations are
by African-American artists.
    ISBN 0-590-48024-3
    1. Christmas—Literary collections.   (1. Christmas—Literary
collections.)   I. Hudson, Cheryl Willis.
  PZ5.H713   1995
  810.8'033--dc20   95-3146
                                                              CIP
                                                               AC

12 11 10 9 8 7 6 5 4 3 2 1   5 6 7 8 9/9 0/0

Printed in the U. S. A.   37
First Scholastic printing, October 1995

Contents

"In day and deed he has no part—
Who holds not Christmas in his heart!"
from *Christmas in the Heart*
by Paul Laurence Dunbar

It's Christmas in the House!

by Mia Watson

Illustrated by Anna Rich

It's Christmas in the house!
It's Christmas in the house!

Jingle bells, cowrie shells—
Shakere! It's Christmas!
Holiday songs, sing-alongs,
Festive times are with us.

It's Christmas in the house!
It's Christmas in the house!

Eggnog and punch,
With fruitcake to munch.
Laughter fills the air.
There's mistletoe,
Perhaps some snow,
And special gifts to share.

4

It's Christmas in the house!
It's Christmas in the house!

Look! Santa's in the sky,
Eating sweet potato pie.
Believe me, now. Don't fuss!
Honor Christ's birth
With peace on earth.
Joy to the world!
It's Christmas.

It's Christmas in the house!
It's Christmas in the house!

Tradition

by Gwendolyn Brooks
Illustrated by Cal Massey

At Home, the buying of the Christmas tree was a ritual. Always it had come into the Brown household four days before Christmas, tall, but not too tall, and not too wide. Tinsel, bulbs, little Santa Clauses and snowmen, and the pretty gold and silver and colored balls did not have to be renewed oftener than once in five years because after Christmas they were always put securely away, on a special shelf in the basement, where they rested for a year. Black walnut candy, in little flat white sheets, crunchy, accompanied the tree, but it was never eaten

until Christmas Eve. Then, late at night, a family decorating party was held, Maud Martha, Helen, and Harry giggling and teasing and occasionally handing up a ball or Santa Claus, while their father smiled benignly over all and strung and fitted and tinseled, and their mother brought in the black walnut candy and steaming cups of cocoa with whipped cream, and plain shortbread. And everything peaceful, sweet!

My Christmas Tree
by Gertrude Parthenia McBrown
Illustrated by Eric Battle

Come, see my pretty Christmas tree;
Oh, I'm as happy as can be.
See my nice, new mamma doll,
And my big, red rubber ball;
All these things around the tree,
Santa brought them here for me.

Midnight Service
by Marguerita Roett
Illustrated by James Ransome

Christina was so excited. She could hardly wait. It was Christmas Eve and this was the first time she would be taken to Midnight Service.

"You're only six years old and you'll get to stay up way past your bedtime," her older sister Kimmie grumbled. "Mommy and Daddy didn't take me to Midnight Service till I was seven. You'll probably fall asleep in the middle of everything anyway."

"I'm not sleepy," Christina said before running off. "I want to help decorate the tree. And I want to go see what smells so good in the kitchen."

"You smell the Christmas cake baking," Kimmie called out matter-of-factly. "And you smell the turkey stuffing cooking, too. When you get to be nine like me, you'll know all these things."

Kimmie frowned. She had forgotten how excited she used to get at Christmastime, when everything was special and new to her. She was annoyed with Christina, who just wouldn't keep still. And Christina asked so many questions. But most of all, she got so much attention from everyone. Kimmie had loved being the center of attention when she was the only little one in the house. Now she had to share *everything* with Christina.

Christina walked back and forth from the living room to the kitchen and then back again. *Why is everyone taking so long to get ready for church?* she said to herself. There was so much hustle and bustle as the grown-ups prepared for the big day. Finally, the family was ready to go to Midnight Service.

"Wow!" Christina said as they turned the last corner, walking toward church. The church and the surrounding trees were all decorated with tiny, white lights. In the darkness outside, Christina thought she must be in Wonderland.

Inside, there were candles on the altar and even a Christmas tree next to the pulpit. Christina sat down in a pew with her family and didn't say a word. She just stared at the beautiful sights. Her eyes beamed with excitement. She heard the organ playing Christmas carols and she sang the songs softly to herself.

*Hark! The herald angels sing, glory to
the newborn king! . . .*

Suddenly, the church was enveloped in darkness. For a moment, only the flickering of hundreds of little lights

could be seen. Long lines of parishioners stood in the aisle holding lighted candles. Christina heard a person with a loud voice read from the Bible, saying,

For unto you is born this day in the city of David, a Savior, which is Christ the Lord. . . .

Then the procession began. One after another, the people with the candles walked slowly down the aisle.

How beautiful! Christina thought. *How wonderful!* She noticed that there were children in the procession. Christina wanted to carry a candle, too.

Before anyone knew what was happening, Christina darted out of her seat and into the aisle. She ran to the head of the marchers and reached for the leader's candle. What could the leader do? He was startled but he didn't say a word. Christina stepped out in front of him holding the candle.

The little girl's face shone brightly in the flickering light. She was so proud and happy to join in the procession. She scarcely noticed the big, wide smiles on the faces of other marchers and people in the congregation. Her big sister Kimmie couldn't help but smile, too. . . .

When it was well past midnight, Christina, six years old, was still wide awake.

All through the holiday, Kimmie never got tired of telling anyone who would listen, "You won't believe what my little sister did at Midnight Service! . . ."

Go, Tell It on the Mountain

Adapted and arranged by John W. Work III
Illustrated by Ron Garnett

Exultant

Refrain

Go, tell it on the moun‑tain, o‑ver the hills and ev‑'ry‑where!

Go, tell it on the moun‑tain that Je‑sus Christ is born._____ While / The / Down

Snow

by Angela Shelf Medearis
Illustrated by Sylvia Walker

Coats on,
boots on,
but no snow.

Small mittens,
long scarves,
but no snow.

The wind howls in.
Trees sway and bend,
but no snow.

Then,
one flake, two flakes.
Snow!

Soon everything
is bright and cold and white.
Snow!

We run outside.
We slip and slide.
Snow!

Arms wave and
angels are made.
Snow!

Snowballs fly.
We duck and hide.
Snow!

We pat and roll
three balls of
snow.

Cold ears, cold hands.
Two eyes, one nose
for the snowman.

Playtime is over.
Good-bye snow.
Time to make
some hot cocoa!

The end

From *Everett Anderson's Year*

by Lucille Clifton

Illustrated by Sylvia Walker

Everett Anderson
in the snow
is a specially
ice-cream boy to know
as he jumps and calls
and spins and falls
with his chocolate nose and
vanilla toes.

Brer Rabbit's Christmas Gift

Adapted by Mia Watson
Illustrated by Eric Battle

*O*nce upon a time there was a sly ol' fox and a friendly but mischievous young rabbit. They had their differences from time to time. But they were neighbors and called each other brother.

Well, it was a crisp, clear winter morning — the day before Christmas, in fact. Brer Fox decided to visit Brer Rabbit's garden. The carrots growing there looked mighty delicious. Brer Rabbit was visiting his friend, Brer Bear, at the time. *Surely, he wouldn't miss a few of those carrots!* At least that's what Brer Fox said to himself.

Well, when Brer Rabbit got home, he was mad as could be. His carrot patch was empty!

"It's that sneaky Brer Fox again!" Brer Rabbit cried out. "He's left his tracks and even some hairs from his bushy tail. I'll get him for this or my name's not B-R-E-R Rabbit!"

Off Brer Rabbit went! *Hippity hop, clippity clip, lickity split!* As he got closer to Brer Fox's house his whiskers twitched. He could smell the delicious aroma of stew coming right from the kitchen.

"Look here, my *bruther*," Brer Rabbit said. "I know those are my carrots you're cooking, so open up the door!"

"Are you nuts?" replied Brer Fox with a cunning smile. "It's Christmas Eve and I don't plan to open my door again until winter is over. No, sir. Thanks to my

kind friend Brer Rabbit, I've got plenty of carrots — for stew, a carrot cake, or whatever. There's a stack of other treats for Christmas dinner, too. The windows are shut tight and the door is bolted. Why don't you take a hike until spring? I want to enjoy my first bowl of carrot stew in peace."

Brer Rabbit got so mad he kicked and punched at the door. And his feet were big, too! *Thumpity thump! Thumpity thump! Blip blop! Blip blam!* But, it was no use. Brer Fox was stubborn and would not open the door.

Brer Rabbit turned and left in a rage! *Hippity hop, clippity clip, lickity split!* "Kind friend, my cotton tail!" Rabbit said. "How dare he?"

Pretty soon Brer Rabbit calmed down, and by the time he reached his own home, he had a plan to get his carrots back and to fix that ol' Fox, too!

Late Christmas Eve night, Brer Rabbit hauled a sack of stones onto his shoulder and climbed onto Brer Fox's roof. *Cling clang, blip bang!* He made plenty of noise.

"Who's that up on my roof?" Fox called out. "Go away, I'm cooking my supper!"

"Ho, Ho, Ho! It's Santa Claus," replied Brer Rabbit in a big fake voice that sounded deep and jolly.

"Well, in that case," said Fox, "come on down. You're very welcome. Just slide down the chimney."

"I can't," said Brer Rabbit. "I'm stuck. Too many gifts!"

Swoosh! Brer Fox ran to the front door, unbolted the lock, and looked up on the roof. He thought he could see someone there with a sack of presents. So he rushed back inside and called out, "Well, Santa, don't bother about trying to come down the chimney yourself! Just drop the sack of presents and I'll catch it."

"I can't!" said Brer Rabbit in his Santa Claus voice. "That's stuck, too. Guess you'll have to climb up, pull the string around the sack, and haul it down for yourself."

"Easy said, easy done," said Brer Fox. And *swoop!* Up he went. Straight up the chimney.

As quick as you could say "Jackie Robinson," Brer Rabbit hopped off that roof and through the open doorway. *Hippity hop, clippity clip, lickety split!*

He gathered the carrots, juice, carrot cake, plus the dressing, a fine cooked goose, and a minced meat pie. He stuffed them into an extra sack and dashed off!

Meanwhile, Brer Fox was just a-climbing up, up, up the chimney. It was dark and he couldn't see, but he could feel the string hanging down. Can you imagine what happened?

Brer Fox pulled on that string and out tumbled all the stones — *Kapong! Blip! Bang!* — right on Brer Fox's head! Christmas gift, indeed!

Fox tumbled and crashed down the chimney, sooty, upset, and sore! Poor Brer Fox! Not only had he lost his Christmas dinner, but he had a great big headache, too.

Brer Rabbit had run so fast that he reached his house before Brer Fox hit the hearth. Rabbit laughed and laughed and laughed at the trick he had played. "Ho, ho, ho! What a Christmas gift!"

Brer Rabbit made sure to stay out of Brer Fox's way all that Christmas Day and for many days to come.

And that's the truth!

Christmas Kittens
by Cheryl Willis Hudson
Illustrated by Higgins Bond

My Christmas kittens
Have soft, fluffy mittens,
Handsome striped coats,
And white fur
'Round their throats.

They play near the tree
With the presents for me.
Each comes with a bow.
They're from Santa, you know.

Carol of the Brown King

by Langston Hughes
Illustrated by Cal Massey

Of the three Wise Men
Who came to the King,
One was a brown man
So they sing.

Of the three Wise Men
Who followed the Star,
One was a brown king
From afar.

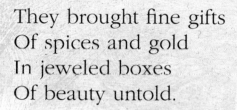

They brought fine gifts
Of spices and gold
In jeweled boxes
Of beauty untold.

Unto this humble
Manger they came
And bowed their heads
In Jesus's name.

Three Wise Men,
One dark like me —
Part of His
Nativity.

Children, Go Where I Send Thee

Black traditional carol
Illustrated by Anna Rich

Spirited

mf

Child-ren, go where I send thee. How will you send me?

cumulative repeat for subsequent verses

I will send you one by one 'Cause one was the lit-tle bit-ty ba - by
I will send you two by two. __ Two was __ Paul and __ Si - las, ... *etc.*

Note:
Sing the verses below in ascending order. The 2-bar repeat is sung in descending order, for cumulative effect.

...I will send you two by two.
Two was Paul and Silas,
One was the little bitty baby,
wrapped in the hollow of a claw horn, etc. ...

Three was the Hebrew children,

Four was the four come a-knockin' at the door,
Five was the gospel preachers,
Six was the six that couldn't get fixed,
Seven was the seven went up to heaven,
Nine was the nine got left behind,
Ten was the ten commandments,

California Christmas

by Toyomi Igus
Illustrated by Ron Garnett

Everyone's idea of Christmastime
doesn't look like Christmas to me.
I've never seen an icicle
or a snow-covered Christmas tree.

I've never gone on a sleighride
or made a real snowman.
But I can ride my skateboard in winter
And make angels in the sand.

All I know is I don't shovel snow before
I can go out to play.
I don't need a coat, boots, or mittens.
And what's an earmuff anyway?

When Santa arrives he must feel hot.
Outside it's 80 degrees!
He'll have to climb in through
our windows
'cause the earthquake broke all our
chimneys.

We decorate our palm trees
with surfing Santas and reindeer.
And we wait for all the grand
marching bands
in the Rose Parade each New Year.

Having snow at Christmastime
would be a sight to see,
But I think a California Christmas
is good enough for me.

Christmas Valentine

by Nikki Grimes
Illustrated by Cal Massey

I asked Mama
what she wanted for Christmas.
"Honey," she said,
"all I want is you."

But I'm way too big to fit under the tree.
So, when she wasn't looking,
I snuck into her sewing room
for scraps of velvet, ribbon, and lace,
and got tracing paper
from out of my desk
and grabbed the glue.

Then, two days later I gave Mama
her very first Christmas Valentine,
with my picture pasted smack in the middle,
and I could swear a tear ran down
her cheek when I said,
"Merry Christmas, Mama."

A Shepherd's Song at Christmas

by Langston Hughes
Illustrated by Ron Garnett

Look there at the star!
I, among the least,
Will arise and take
A journey to the East.
But what shall I bring
As a present for the King?
What shall I bring to the Manger?
        I will bring a song,
        A song that I will sing,
        In the Manger.

Watch out for my flocks,
Do not let them stray.
I am going on a journey
Far, far away.
But what shall I bring
As a present for the Child?
What shall I bring to the Manger?
        I will bring a lamb,
        Gentle, meek, and mild,
        A lamb for the Child
        In the Manger.

I'm just a shepherd boy.
Very poor I am —
But I know there is
A King in Bethlehem.
What shall I bring
As a present just for Him?
What shall I bring to the Manger?

I will bring my heart
And give my heart to Him.
I will bring my heart
To the Manger.

Christmas

Lively

Refrain A

Christ-mas is a-com-in' and it's a-jump-in',

A   E7   A

Christ-mas is a-com-in' and it's a-jump-in', Christ-mas is a-com-in'

E7   A

and it's a-jump-in', Boys, twelve feet long. ___

Verse   D

Chick-en crows at mid-night on a Christ-mas Day,
Child-ren get ___ so hap-py on a Christ-mas Day,

E7   A   *D.C.*

Roost-er crows at mid-night on a Christ-mas Day,
Child-ren get ___ so hap-py on a Christ-mas Day.

is a-comin'

by Huddie Ledbetter
Illustrated by Anna Rich

Refrain

Santa Claus a-comin' and he's a-comin',
Santa Claus a-comin' and he's a-comin',
Boys, twelve feet long.

Verses

Santa Claus is a-comin' on Christmas, on a Christmas Day,
Santa Claus is a-comin' on Christmas, on a Christmas Day,

Children run and shout to pappy on a Christmas Day,
Children run and shout to pappy on a Christmas Day,

Little children get so happy on a Christmas Day,
Little children get so happy on a Christmas Day.

New Year's Wish
by Cheryl Willis Hudson
Illustrated by Cal Massey

Wish simply this:
To have the smarts
To save a part
Of Christmas
In your heart.